Margaret Cameron
New Zealand 1984

Primitive Art of the New Zealand Maori

GLEN POWNALL

Primitive art of the New Zealand Maori

SEVEN SEAS PUBLISHING PTY LIMITED
Wellington and Sydney

Frontispiece: Hollow sculpture

Photography by KIM GOLDWATER, LLOYD HOMER, *and* RICHARD SILCOCK

ISBN 85467 013 0

© 1972 Seven Seas Publishing Pty Limited,
2nd Printing 1979
Wellington, New Zealand
Printed in Hong Kong by
Dai Nippon Printing Co., (Hong Kong) Ltd

Contents

SECTION 1   THE MAORI AND THEIR ART   13

The transition of Maori art
The tohunga's place in Maori culture
The turning point of the Maori race
Pre-contact and traditional Maori art

SECTION 2   THE MAORI AS AN ARTIST   17

Themes in Maori art
The chief motifs of primitive Maori art
Sexual elements in early Maori art
The impact of European technology on Maori culture
Pre-contact Maori dress
Omissions from this book

CHAPTER 1   THE IMAGINATIVE MAORI   24

CHAPTER 2   STYLES OF DRESS   36

CHAPTER 3   WAR AND RECREATION   46

CHAPTER 4   ANCESTOR REVERENCE   56

CHAPTER 5   DOMESTIC ART FORMS   66

CHAPTER 6   ART OUTDOORS   80

Preface

To teach is to learn; to write of matters of personal concern is to be introspective. There is an empathy between New Zealanders and their country; an empathy which makes our land, and all that it denotes, of great importance to us.

In producing this book my feelings for my country resulted in an intense desire to present a true picture of the original New Zealanders; the Maori people who dwelt where I now dwell, a thousand years or more before my ancestors came to share their culture with that of the folk who met them on the shores.

The picture that can be drawn at this distance in time of the pre-contact Maori is hazy. There is so much we don't know, so very much distortion, such a wealth of information wrongly interpreted, that it will take years of scholarship before we can expect to be able to see clearly the Maori as he really was.

What we do have are examples of the material culture of the Maori, the artifacts and tools of trade; remnants of their clothing; articles of artistic merit and religious significance. We also have a few, a very few, faithful people who value truth above sentiment and have the knowledge and experience to judge what may be original Maori work and what is probably tainted with European influence.

The task of offering genuine knowledge of the pre-contact Maori becomes simple in concept but difficult in execution.

Hundreds of colour photographs were taken of supposedly genuine pre-European Maori materials. Then each photograph was examined and where the evidence was unquestionable that the article existed before any European reached New Zealand, that photograph was placed in a pile for possible incorporation in this book.

A second pile included that material which apparently was created after European contact was made.

The first pile, the genuine pre-contact work grew slowly; the reject pile grew fast.

A complication arose, the genuine material lacked variety in some respects. Among all the authentic work, time and natural attrition had produced a certain sameness. Put together they presented a somewhat one-sided picture, as if a future civilization were to judge our contemporary world using as evidence of our society the work of post-impressionist artists alone.

A compromise was essential if anything like the balanced picture was to be presented. Hence, there has been included, a certain amount of material which probably originated during the contact period but (and this is a very important but) every reasonable precaution which we could adopt has been taken to ensure that the mode of workmanship, the technique of production, the material and the final artistic style of every article featured in this book would be recognised and accepted by a pre-contact Maori as a natural and normal part of his contemporary culture. With this I must be satisfied.

GLEN POWNALL, *Carterton*, 7/12/1971

Introduction

From the late 18th century on, Europeans began to make an increasingly significant impact on the society and culture of the endemic Maori race of New Zealand.

From the moment of Captain Cook's first visit to this country in 1769 the Maori felt the influence of Europeans, explorers, sealers and whalers; followed by missionaries and settlers. The changes they brought to Maori life and customs continue to this day, over two hundred years beyond the initial contact date.

It is difficult to have a true understanding today of events so far removed in time and so poorly documented, but the effects of the introduction of a foreign technology did have a profound influence on the Maori race. The early history of the colonization of New Zealand has written into it a mass of myth and mis-information, even propaganda, all biased in favour of European interests.

The Maoris themselves had no written language and as will be explained later, had reason to neglect their own continuity of history. Hence a large measure of the knowledge of old New Zealand has come to us through sources other than the Maori.

Within the last five to ten years some local ethnologists with training in anthropology have taken a fresh look at the Maori in a more objective way than past investigators have done. Many New Zealanders have become apologists when explaining the differences which exist between Maori and European and propagandists for a cult of equality without any real understanding as to what equality in this context implies. Sentiment rather than sense has coloured the relationship between Maori and European in the past and sentiment continues to give rise to faulty judgments in the field of Maori culture and art.

The complex factors affecting reactions between two peoples from different cultures have, in New Zealand, not been as serious in end result as in other countries and the outcome of the mixing of two ethnic groups has been a feeling of mutual indifference. Some Maori have become thoroughly Europeanised, whilst others have not successfully made the transition to the European dominated economic world, or are hostile or indifferent to it.

Indifference does not lead to a good working partnership where members of a total society are anxious to preserve their own separate identities.

It is important however that individual New Zealanders recognise that they have a common heritage in Maori art and culture, even though this heritage may originate only from the forbears of the Maori section of our community.

The outward signs of the inner life of a society are in the art forms of that people. A change in social or cultural mores will be reflected in a change in the position of art in the community and in the form and content of that art. So it has been in New Zealand. What is generally accepted today as Maori art in the traditional manner, is with very few exceptions, grotesque, over-embellished, sometimes quaint and of far more interest as tourist trade fodder than as a source of inspiration and communication between people.

Beauty and simplicity are implicit in the work we know of the Maori of pre-European times. As the illustrations in this book show, the pre-contact Maori artist was a master of his media, with an appreciation of form and design quite equal to that shown in any of the recognised great periods of art elsewhere. It is unfortunate that the New Zealand climate and the original Maori way of life did not permit the preservation of the more delicate materials for which one can find some reference in the literature of the earliest voyagers. Hence several hundreds of years after the death of the artist we can make our judgments only where the work was rendered in long lasting species of timber, stone and the semi-permanent bones of animals and men.

There has been a very great wastage of pre-contact Maori art and artifacts. Most of this loss has been occasioned by natural causes and the non-realisation of its value. A considerable number of artifacts are known to have been wilfully destroyed by over-zealous missionaries who, through ignorance, burnt and broke up irreplaceable objects under the mistaken impression that they were freeing potential converts from the temptation to keep on worshipping graven images.

Nevertheless the amount of material still in existence and known with some degree of certainty to be free of European influence is very considerable. This book is an attempt to display for the first time in one volume a great number of pre-contact Maori pieces. It is offered as a tribute to primitive artists who flourished in a stone age culture, and whose work remains as an inspiration to New Zealanders today.

1 | The Maori and their art

For two hundred years anthropologists and others have asked the question from whence came the root stock of the proto-Polynesians who spread their descendents into the islands of the Pacific, but not to Australia and South America? Where too was the land the Polynesian people recognised as their legendary homeland, their Hawaiki, and was it by accident or design that the Maori people came and partly colonised the land of New Zealand so very far to the south of where the rest of their race dwelt?

Today interest in the ancient Maori does not rest solely on his origin, but on the fact that by the time of the first European contact, the Maori of New Zealand had evolved customs and a culture very different from any found elsewhere in Polynesia. There was and there still is evident, a great deal of similarity between the Maori and other Polynesians, but the differences outweigh the similarities.

The pre-European Maori lived in a stone age technology with all the limitations imposed by inadequate tools and lack of raw materials. They lacked a written language and never needed a precise vocabulary of measurement. Considered in today's terms, the Maori suffered many handicaps, yet lived in a balanced society. Granted he did, of necessity, live in a relatively unfriendly climate with a food supply that was adequate only by the application of much effort, considerable ingenuity and the possession of a high degree of intelligence.

Rather than just existing on the land, the Maori rose superior to the challenge of their country and developed a society with a highly ethical basis. Kinship was the key to pre-European Maori society and still plays an important part in the lives of their descendents. Their political system is not really understood today, but it may perhaps be summed up as a hereditary autocracy with overtones of communism. If this sound formidible it shouldn't, for the basis of government was a religion supported aristocracy, passing its powers from one generation to the next, but with all goods held in common and with every tribal member having the right to require their leaders to prove themselves capable of leadership.

The early Maori people were divided into a number of territorially autonomous communities with tribal membership measured by descent from a common ancestor and rank graded in accordance with seniority. Sub-tribes occupied out-settlements of the tribal lands and were subservient to the paramount chief's authority.

The transition of Maori art

Every activity in which the Maori engaged had religious connotations. This is a point of the very greatest significance in any understanding of the Maori way of life. The Maori completely integrated this spiritual and temporal existence. In every way the spirit world impacted and permeated into his smallest act. There wasn't any dividing line between his communication with his gods or ancestors and his dealings with his fellows; each was a fact of his very being as a Maori.

Mission religion was not an adequate substitute for the Maori's previous spiritual beliefs, especially as the new religion involved adopting a new social system. This fact has been consciously or sub-consciously overlooked by most historians. Missionary influence was strong in early New Zealand. To the Maori of that time the golden gateway to the pleasures and artifacts of the European appeared to be in the adoption of Christian beliefs which enabled one to behave and dress as a European. The writer is of the strong opinion that few if any of the early Maori converts became believers in the Christian sense. However, in subscribing to Christian ritual the Maori infringed his own spirituality and lost the essence of the identification which he enjoyed with his ancestral gods and his world. The need to simultaneously be involved in two incompatible credences led inevitably to an ambivalence which has never been understood by either European or Maori. This basic spiritual irresolution produced a communication problem between the two races which remains a serious bar to mutual understanding even to this day.

The tohunga's place in Maori culture

The tohunga of the Maori has been equated with the priests of Christian sects and this assumption is incorrect. The Maori had no need of any specialist in communication between his gods and himself. The tohunga of the tribe was really a specially skilled person in one department of life or another. Simply because any temporal action was accompanied by a direct spiritual reaction, a tohunga was a medium in the religious ritual connected with his speciality. To this extent a tohunga was the focal point of certain acts of religious significance. The bigotry of many early missionaries interpreted the spiritual content of a tohunga's action as a direct challenge to the authority of the Christian church and as soon as European dominance was established, Tohungaism was formally outlawed by governmental act. It is quite ludicrous that only within recent years has this act been repealed.

The banning of the practice of Tohungaism and the oftimes savage way the law was enforced helped ensure the collapse of Maori culture. The very basis of Maori life was subverted and the substitution of a religion based on the competitive outlook of a European civilization only partly compensated for the loss. Unquestionably the Maori of the nineteenth century became bewildered, dissatisfied and extreme in their efforts to adjust to their new situation.

As stated earlier, art forms reflect the inner life of a people and along with the collapse of Maori culture came a loss of artistic integrity. The strength and simplicity of classical Maori design yielded to the fussy over elaboration dear to the heart of the Victorian age European who dominated the Maori throughout the last century. It is these debased forms which are generally accepted as depicting Maori art today.

The turning point of the Maori race

The Maori race suffered a calamitous diminution in numbers during the nineteenth century. The introduction of the musket changed their inter-tribal skirmishes into a series of bloody massacres. Traditionally the flower of Maori masculinity led the tribes into battle. In fact Maori politics required that only the most capable exponents of the art of life in totality were allowed in the forefront of battle. Thus the most capable, most intelligent and superior males were the first victims of the musket balls of the new type warfare. The outbreak of a series of wars against Europeans was even more serious in results. The Maori population of today has only just equalled in numbers those living before the Maori wars.

Thus the late nineteenth century saw a drastic drop in population from war and from the effect of European introduced diseases against which the Maori had no natural immunity. Alcohol also wrought havoc amidst a people unused to its effects. The total sum of these deleterious introductions of European culture was that the Maori almost ceased to exist as a racial group.

A people struggling to exist cannot afford the luxury of a proud past. The business of just continuing to live can become so desperate that merely living from one day to the next is an all consuming task. The realization that extermination was just around the corner must have proved a traumatic experience to those who survived, and tradition and ancestral culture necessarily played a very small part in their lives. Therefore the culture and situation of the Maori people at the end of the nineteenth century was very different to that of their pre-European ancestors.

It necessarily followed that the possibility of an understanding and knowledge of pre-contact culture passed largely through foreign missionaries and settlers who simply had neither the background nor the will to recognise the artistic achievements of the people they had nearly killed off. The efforts of well disposed men from a European culture who recorded their own impressions of things Maori actually count for little. Thus, have the misunderstandings, the misconceptions and the very traditions of classical Maori culture, filtered through to our generation via the prejudices of the Victorian age.

Pre-contact and traditional Maori art

The ethnologist of today possesses a healthy scepticism towards the acceptance of the beliefs of early historians of the Maori. Many, if not all, of the accepted authorities of the past are suspect, in that they gave insufficient attention to testing what was told to them, and did not confirm that material they saw was indeed pre-contact and uninfluenced by European thought. This scepticism has forced a new look at Maori cultural traditions and raised a number of doubts as to the genuineness of many of the Maori crafts which have generally been believed to have an unbroken connection with the distant past.

That the Maori of today is the inheritor of some very great art is unquestioned, and the proof of the greatness of the Maori as an artist is pictured in this book. However, where the roots of the so called Maori art of today actually lie is a very different story. Many of the contemporary Maori crafts have artistic merit, but it is questionable as to how far it is possible to say that these crafts are traditional.

As stated previously, a serious attempt has been made to ensure that the objects illustrated in this book are free from European influence and can therefore be regarded as being genuine traditional art forms of a people still untouched by western cultural ideals. It must be emphasised again that the criteria used for selection has been based on the need to show as wide a variety of objects as possible, plus the wish to illustrate the artistic merit of the people under discussion, but, over-riding both these desires has been a determination to reject any objects which might display a European influence.

The importance attached to the illustration of genuine pre-contact material therefore allows comparison to be made between true Maori art themes and those craft elements which are today regarded as being representative of Maori tradition. In effect there is a much lower degree of correlation between pre-contact and contemporarily used motifs than one would expect. It is not proposed to carry out a detailed discussion on this point, but for example early Maori work uses the spiral motif to a much lesser extent than might reasonably be expected, pre-contact designs are much simpler and less static than contemporary craft work and so on.

In one way, the old time Maori artist was as contemporary as the craftworker of today. Modern art, the abstraction of the essence of a shape, an event, an experience, had been anticipated by several centuries by Maori artists whose art was part of their lives. The use of more than one of our senses in the communication of artistic feelings, in that the shape and feel of early Maori work is both a visual and tactile experience, predates by a very long time the modern resurgence of tactile art. Unquestionably the primitive Maori artist has left behind him much work that is inspirational to all who see merit in artistic expression.

2 | The Maori as an artist

The one thing that can be said with truth is that no great work of art is purposeless, a great artist always has a message to communicate, a purpose to fulfil. So it must have been with the Maori artists of the classical and pre-classical periods prior to 1800 A.D.

The art forms shown in this book are timeless and largely homeless. They are timeless because they originated over a long period of racial history lasting probably for a thousand years or more and we cannot tell the order in which the various articles were developed. They are homeless for while all the articles came from New Zealand it is often only the place where they were found that is known. The early Maori people were far from a homogeneous race, being divided into comparatively isolated communities, and there can be no way of knowing in which part of the country a given article originated before being carried to its place of discovery.

As well as being timeless and homeless, the purpose for which the art content was developed is not proven. A great deal of information is offering on pre-European Maori culture. Unquestionably much of what is recorded is real truth, but, increasingly in recent years a considerable portion of what has been held to be true in the past is no longer held to be so. This of course is the progress of knowledge.

Themes in Maori art

It is therefore difficult to speculate on the motives of Maori artists but sufficient is known of the life of the pre-European Maori people for some interesting inferences to be drawn as to why themes in Maori art developed. It is curious that the Maori never developed a written language of even the most elementary form, for lineage was an important social distinction and ancestral records of considerable consequence. To some extent Maori art forms substituted for written records in that certain aspects of ancestral or tribal history were incorporated into the work and thus gave a continuity to the themes expressed over a number of generations. Some attributes of ancestor worship also crept into art. Ancestors could become minor deities. Remote ancestors tended to be pictured in highly stylized forms. There are a number of such figures occurring in Maori art.

The gods of the Maori people, too, had their place in the underlying motives that produced art forms. The ancient Maori found cause to propitiate a hierachy of gods. The Maori cosmogony is complex in its recital of the various stages of evolution from primeval darkness to the coming of light and the development of man. The hegemony included, Rangi—the sky and the senior male ancestor; Papa, the earth mother; Tangaroa, the all important god of the sea and ocean; Rongo, agriculture; Tane, forests; Tawhirimatea, storms; Ru, earthquakes, volcanoes and the underworld—a very fierce, powerful and jealous god; Tu, war; together with a number of others, some of which were local tribal gods. Some anthropologists rank the local or district gods at the third level of importance, but these deities are with few exceptions personifications of natural phenomena as with Rangi, Papa and Tane.

Definitely of less importance than the major gods were the demons, the spirits, deified ancestors and other dwellers of the spirit world. However in many ways these spiritual beings were of more immediate importance in everyday affairs than the loftier upper echelons. Demons, spirits and departed ancestors took a close interest in worldly affairs and could and would interfere in the most minor activities of life. Virtually every object, tool, artifact and operation was subject to the attention of one or more spirit.

It is possible, even probable, that so much of the embellishment on artifacts and most of what we now recognise as artwork had its conception in the wish of the artist to propitiate and glorify one or more of the spirits who shared his world with him. Great art has been produced for far less noble motives.

A measure of the sophistication demonstrated by the ancient Maori in his theology is the almost complete absence of images of religious significance. Image worship was not a part of Maori beliefs. While the Maori attitude towards his gods is now a matter of speculation there is reason to believe that in certain directions he exhibited a somewhat cynical tolerance in regard to the intelligence displayed by the minor gods and spirits.

Above all the Maori was a realist in his religious beliefs. Prayers were all powerful. Recite the correct prayer and the god to whom the prayer was addressed had no option but to answer the request. Failure of a god to action a correctly stated prayer was failure as a god and that god was promptly replaced by another more willing to respond to propitiation. The Maori also recognised the need to honour and give some recompense to a god who served him faithfully and well and it was common to offer the god a dwelling place or habitation in the form of a god stick (a carved wooden form) or one of the so called kumara gods. The sweet potato, or kumara, was the staple starch food of the pre-European Maori. Such was the importance of this crop in the Maori economy that special ceremonies and acts to invoke the protection of the gods had to be undertaken during planting and subsequent cultivation of the plant. In order to attract benevolent spirits and cause them to remain in the vicinity of the growing crop it was a usual custom to erect crude shrines or resting places for the deities on the boundaries of the cultivated area. These shrines were sometimes carved from stone in a very crude resemblance of a human figure. Little care was apparently taken to make the images in the real likeness of the human form. The term now used, i.e. kumara god, is a misnomer for these figures, since they were only the temporary dwelling place of the gods and during the off-season were removed from the fields and stored away with little ceremony or reverence.

The chief motifs of primitive Maori art

A traditional feature shown in one form or another in nearly every old time Maori carving is the figure generally known as the manaia. There is considerable variation in the design of manaia figures. In some cases a highly stylised representation of the human is shown. More commonly the resemblence favours that of a bird. Some of the oldest manaia have lizard characteristics while quite a number of the figures are so highly abstract as to bear no likeness to any known object or animal. The obvious desire of the artist is to portray something so strange as to be awe inspiring. It is characteristic of manaia that the design is shown side face and that the details are formalised, lizard features being indicated by exaggerated four-toed feet, while eyes and mouth parts are simplified to circles. The type of primitive art represented by manaia is common to many countries and anthropologists have speculated on the possible connection between similar designs found in widely separated places, but such evidence that offers to support theories of ancestral memories and pre-historic migrations is tenuous at the best. However it is curious that the New Zealand Maori, living in an area where no fossil records of snakes have ever been found, should depict some of their more horrifying figures as possessing forked tongues.

The spiral patterns of Maori art are a considerable departure from the generally straight line, geometric patterns of the rest of the Polynesian peoples. The simple spiral pattern or koru, is a common element in primitive art throughout the world but the Maori artist developed double spirals, 'S' curve spirals, interlocking spirals and variations of these basic forms. The spiral form is a distinctive feature of post-European Maori art, but plays a far less important part in the earlier Maori forms such as are being discussed in this book.

It is apparent that the early Maori artists were reflecting a highly virile, active society. The accent in almost every piece of work was on rhythm. Movement was an integral part of design, where the flowing rhythm of the design required it, the theme was repeated, and if this repetition led to the formalization of some design element, this was done. If it seemed right to the artist to link his rhythm into spiral curves of one sort or another then spirals resulted as a natural consequence. However, even a fairly cursory study of some of the more elaborate designs shown in this book, will prove that in the classical and pre-classical periods, many other motifs for the repetition of design were as favoured as were spiral patterns.

In-so-far as these artists appeared to wish to portray a dynamic and virile society, one cannot but admire the true artistry displayed in showing both rhythm and movement within the limits imposed by the bone, wood and stone with which they were working. It has been claimed that Maori culture, as depicted by their art forms, was static and stultified, but this is not borne out by the examples shown in this book. In illustration after illustration is seen the artistic ability, albeit licence, to place the head of a figure in an unnatural position in order that the swelling rhythm of a design be maintained or to bend the limbs into a flowing pattern to continue the sense of movement. It is true that post-classical work tends to lack this movement, and, if so, it is but a reflection of the loss of self-identification the Maori people underwent at the time.

Perhaps the most outstanding feature of Maori art is the frequent occurrence of distorted human figures, a characteristic shared in common with most primitive art. The human head was often shown as exaggerated in size, with more careful attention given to detail than to other parts of the body. It is known that the ancient Maori regarded the head as more sacred, more tapu, than the rest of the body. In many cases the mouth is shown open, with the tongue lolling and the eyes protruding. The whole facial gestures are of defiance and mirror the grimaces which warriors customarily employed during war dances (haka).

A hand with three fingers occurs in most old carved figures. There are variations, sometimes three fingers and a thumb, elsewhere a thumb and two fingers only. There seems to be no commonly accepted reason for this convention. Some anthropologists claim that it is a remnant of a racial memory, going far back into proto-human times and common also to Europe, Japan, Peru, Greece and India. Others interpret the mystic origin of the three-fingered hand in terms of an old Maori myth. This myth refers to one Nuku-wai-teko, a Maori folk hero who first taught the art of carving. He had been born with only three fingers on each hand and in his honour all images were so depicted ever after. A third alternative attributes the convention of a three-fingered hand to the desire to make the images somewhat less than human. On balance this is in keeping with other aspects of Maori cultural art. The desire seems to have been to depict the spirit of the object rather than impart realism.

The lizard is worthy of special mention in connection with Maori carving for the reason that it was the only figure carved with any degree of realism. There has been considerable speculation over this reluctance to deform the lizard's shape. It could well be that the association of the lizard with Whiro, the god who held command of evil and death, makes the lizard such a dread figure that there was no need to introduce grotesque distortions to enhance its frightening aspects.

The primitive Maori, both men and women, used ornaments for personal adornment. The huia (an extinct bird) provided a black feather with a pure white tip which was especially prized as a head ornament. Anklets were worn by women, and both sexes wore ear pendants, necklaces of shell, shark teeth and berries. Shark teeth, whilst popular, did not rate as highly as did human teeth.

Nephrite or greenstone ornaments were classed among the most valuable of the few possessions owned by an individual Maori. This high value is understandable considering the difficulty in obtaining greenstone, it being found in a very few comparatively inaccessible places in the South Island.

By far the best known ornament as far as contemporary New Zealanders are concerned is the tiki, or more correctly heitiki. Judging by the number of genuine examples of the tiki that still exist, it must have been a highly prized and very popular personal adornment. Tiki were pendants invariably made with a hole in the upper edge for the attachment of a thong or plaited cord so that they could be suspended around the neck of the wearer. In form the tiki represented the full-face figure of a human being, a familiar theme in Maori art, and complementary to the side-face or manaia form of human beings. Thus the tiki as a design element and the heitiki as personal ornaments show considerable development and much variation.

Sexual elements in early Maori art

Early Maori work gives strong emphasis to primary sexual characteristics. As with all peoples, the Maori was concerned with life and death and not unnaturally associated this with male and female sexuality. The early missionaries strongly disapproved of both the sexual and religious elements in Maori culture and not only took active steps to displace both from art work, but undoubtedly destroyed much art which displayed such subversion to the doctrines they were promoting.

The impact of European technology on Maori culture

The impact of European culture on later Maori carvers has been substantial, particularly in the development of more elaborate designs with a greater amount of secondary embellishment than used by earlier carvers. This may have been encouraged by the greater convenience and lesser effort required in carving with steel tools in contrast to the bone and stone tools previously used.

The carving of stone and bone artifacts virtually ceased with the coming of the European, until its re-introduction as a commercial enterprise to serve a tourist trade well into the twentieth century.

The Maori produced hard wearing fabrics from the fibres of a number of plants. Most commonly used was the long, strong, lustrous fibres of the Phormium tenax plant (which is sometimes known as the New Zealand flax). After considerable scraping and retting of the raw leaf, flax yields a very high quality fibre capable of being woven into strong fabrics.

Maori methods of weaving were, from the modern point of view, extremely crude and time consuming, and at no stage reached the degree of sophistication of some races even more primitive in cultural background.

The weaving loom, if the crude apparatus in use can be elevated to the distinction of a loom, consisted of a strong cord tied horizontally between two posts set firmly in the ground. A series of warp threads were tied to the horizontal cord and allowed to dangle free. The horizontal weft threads were then worked by hand between the vertical warp threads. The whole process demonstrates an extremely low level of technology and it is hard to imagine a more tedious way of producing cloth. Despite the severe limitations of the methods used, amazingly good quality fabric was produced and some extremely intricate patterns incorporated therein, using a peculiar Maori method of finger plaiting known as taniko weaving. Some examples of patterns produced in pre-European times have survived and are shown pictured later.

New Zealand's first major export was in dried human heads. These Maori heads had considerable commercial value apart from their obvious scientific interest. Sealers and other itinerant early visitors were not averse to making an honest dollar or pound in satisfying the morbid interest of their stay-at-home fellow countrymen by offering such wares. The feature that made these dried human heads such a highly marketable commodity was the tattoos placed thereon at the will of the original owner of the head. Probably nowhere else in the world did human tattooing reach the degree of popularity that it enjoyed in primitive

New Zealand society. It may be added that the face was not the only part of the body adorned with tattoos, at least in the case of the male, but certainly it was the only part exported.

Tattooed designs were very elaborate, duplicating the curvilinear shapes of wood carvings. The method of impressing the design was painful and of great significance. High tapu surrounded the performance which was carried out by priests of high rank and a ceremonial feast concluded the ordeal.

Tattooing operations were carried out in a temporary shelter erected out-of-doors in an area which was then declared tapu. Elaborately carved handles carried a variety of chisels. Usually made of bone (albatross bone being very popular), the chisel, which was seated into the handle, was ground flat and furnished with a cutting edge up to a quarter of an inch or even more in width. The operator traced the design and the chisel was dipped into a mixture of soot and plant juice. The prepared chisel was then placed in position and the cutting edge driven through the skin with a sharp blow on the back of the instrument.

Both men and women were tattooed, although female tattoo was generally restricted to lips and chin, while the male had face, thighs and buttocks adorned. Tattoo designs varied considerably even at the time of European observation. It is not known with any degree of certainty how tattoo designs should be interpreted. It appears reasonable to suppose that the lines and patterns represented something more than personal adornment and it has been held by some students of Maori social customs that tattoo marks showed both the lineage and military honours of the wearer.

Pre-contact Maori dress

The so-called traditional Maori dress of today bears little resemblance to that of the pre-European Maori. Once again the Victorian influence is seen and particularly that of the missionaries. The more prudish of the early voyagers deplored the lack of dress of the natives they saw and there is now a wide divergence of opinion among ethnologists as to what constituted the everyday wear of people of that time. Certainly a lot of work has lately been carried out on the derivation and classification of Maori dress as such, but it must be remembered that one is talking about more than one thousand years of history and the task of placing changes in dress fashion in order becomes almost impossible. However, some examples of what are believed to be genuine Maori modes of dressing are given in the appropriate chapter.

Omissions from this book

Any New Zealander will note large sections of what are regarded as traditional Maori work missing from this book. There is no tuku-tuku or reed panel work; no carved meeting houses; no painted rafter patterns; no piu-piu or grass skirts—these are all conscious omissions since there is no firm evidence that these articles are indeed pre-European. There are other and quite genuine areas of pre-European art and craft which have been regretfully left out for lack of space. However the aim of this book is not to give an exhaustive treatment of classical and pre-classical Maori art but merely to give prominence for the first time in a popular book to the work of many fine artists who deserve a much wider audience than has tended to be the case previously.

PLATE 1/1 *Wooden sculptured figure*
The primitive New Zealand Maori artist seldom portrayed the human figure in any realistic detail. This example possibly approaches realism as nearly as was ever depicted in pre-contact times.

CHAPTER ONE

The imaginative Maori

Human beings quite naturally are interested in other human beings and all primitive art has as its major element the expression of people and their activities. A primitive people lives much closer to the basic facts of life than do we in our sophisticated contemporary society; life and death have a greater immediacy to them than to us; and their spiritual and temporal existences are less well defined than are ours.

The New Zealand Maori had greater pre-occupation with the depiction of the human form in his art than is perhaps the case with other peoples in primitive societies. Man, in early New Zealand was the only living enemy of other human beings. There were no carnivorous animals larger than insects dwelling here.

The Polynesian race, of which the Maori are a branch, shared in common a reverence for the memory of honoured ancestors and leaders. With the Maori this ancestor veneration was compounded by a social force known as mana which has no synonymous equivalent in the English language.

Mana was one manifestation of a psychic force that gave to its possessors, power, prestige, authority, the ability to succeed in all aspects of life and even gave some control over spiritual beings. Mana was in the first instance conferred by the accident of being born into the right ancestral line, although the possessor had to maintain his own mana by his personal actions throughout life. Mana was the most cherished possession of a Maori. Thus to display a symbolic representation of an ancestor of high mana was to proclaim one's own or one's tribal mana. This preoccupation with mana lead to the depiction of the human figure in sculptured forms, from comparatively realistic facsimiles to highly abstract, and this is the order we have followed in this section. Abstraction and symbolism, to the point where the human basis of the sculpture is difficult to recognise, is believed to represent the interfusion of the spiritual and temporal life of the Maori. Lizard-like characteristics probably related to life, bird-like forms referred to the transition towards after-life, and the human semblance introduced humanity.

PLATE 1/2 *Carved wooden figure*
Defiance was a prime quality in the personification of Maori male virility. The unknown artist of this figure has admirably incorporated this attitude into his work.

Plates 1/1, 1/16, 1/17 by courtesy of Dominion Museum, Wellington.
Plates 1/2–1/8, 1/10–1/15, 1/18, 1/19 by courtesy of Auckland War Memorial Museum.
Plate 1/9 by courtesy of Wanganui Public Museum.

PLATE 1/3 *Stone sculpture*
The difficulty of working fine detail into stone while using stone tools was immense. This chunky statue overcomes in its artistic quality the limitations of the tools and techniques.

PLATE 1/4 *Wooden bone-box*
Probably intended to hold the skull of an honoured ancestor, this hollow wooden sculpture possesses a clever grotesque cast of feature still capable of commanding attention several hundred years after it was carved.

PLATE 1/5 *Entwined wooden figures*
The incorporation of vibrant life as the essence of the art of living is a feature of much pre-contact Maori art. This detail from a carved lintel is a tribute to a great artist's understanding of his people.

1/3

1/4

1/5

PLATE 1/6 *Carved wooden figure*
This commanding figure, which dominates the central position of the elaborate carved design shown in part in plate 1/5, exemplifies some of the characteristics early missionaries found so distasteful that they caused the destruction of similar work. The primary sexual characteristic undoubtedly had esoteric significance to the early Maori, equivalent to 'In the midst of life we face death.'

PLATES 1/7 & 1/8 *Canoe prow and detail*
Apparently of very early execution, the manaia figure shown in detail in plate 1/8 was once the carved figurehead of a canoe. The distortion of the human profile probably was intended to convey menace.

PLATE 1/9 *Sinuous figure*
This figure, a magnificently executed example of primitive art, is surface carved from a plank of wood and shows the absolute mastery of an artist in imparting a timelessness to writhing movement.

1/7

1/8

1/9

PLATES 1/10 & 1/11 *Sculptured composition*
These beautifully proportioned examples of the wood carver's art were possibly once a decorative piece mounted on the roof of a very ancient dwelling or mortuary house. A magnificent example of rhythmic abstraction in wood.

PLATE 1/12 *Detail from plate 1/10*
The manaia figure from the extremity of the sculptured composition in plate 1/10 accents the sense of balance of the whole piece and the near ultimate in the stylization of the human profile.

1/11

1/10

PLATE 1/13 *Central figure from plate 1/10*
A mastery of portrayal of the artist's interpretation of humanity is depicted in this fully sculptured figure which is the central element of the whole composition.

PLATE 1/14 *Relief figure*
Advancing further towards pure abstraction this detail (from the lintel shown in full in plate 1/5) retains a degree of humanity while yielding to the desire of the artist to infuse the essence of his medium (wood) with that of his subject (man).

PLATE 1/15 *Abstract figure*
From the same lintel the artist has moved further towards formalization while turning the face of the figure almost into profile, yet not losing his theme.

PLATES 1/16 & 1/17 *Heitiki*
These two beautifully executed examples of heitiki have been grouped to show the subtlety of design that the primitive Maori artist could incorporate into his work. These two examples were executed in translucent nephrite, a favourite medium.

PLATES 1/18 & 1/19 *Stone carvings*
Hard, intractable, tough, fibrous, and just plain difficult are all adjectives which have been justly applied to the New Zealand member of the jade family, the pounamu or greenstone of the Maori; the nephrite of the contemporary scientist. Yet from this obstinate stone were created these two whimsically delightful figures. They are shown here on adjoining pages so that the artistic expression, the licence to follow the natural characteristics of a difficult material, are exemplified in full. Here are two figures which while being so very different have at the same time a great deal in common. Who can doubt the humanity of a people whose artists created work such as this?

1/19

CHAPTER TWO

Styles of dress

Intermarriage between Maori and European has been freely practised since the earliest contact period. The favour of women was a highly successful trade item offered in return for coveted European goods and artifacts. The result has been that Maori of pure Polynesian descent are very few in numbers today. This results in our inability to pronounce with certainty on the physical appearance of the primitive Maori. From the journals of early voyagers it is certain that the undiluted Maori race was of fine physique, but accounts of the attractiveness of their features vary considerably. When one recalls the length of time the chroniclers had been at sea the possibility of impartial judgment would not be great anyway.

However we do know that the contemporary Maori is handsome as will be noted from the people who are modelling the clothing of their ancestors. It should perhaps be said here that reliable accounts of the way in which women's clothing was worn are almost non-existent and the methods of wearing shown in this section may not be completely authentic.

It is certain that the ancestors of the Maori migrated from an area nearer the equator than New Zealand and that these early migrants had to adapt to new materials and the need for more clothing. The New Zealand native flax plant, Phormium tenax, yields after scraping, treating and pounding, a fibre of excellent quality. It became the basic material from which Maori clothing was produced.

The usual protective garment was of woven flax fibre and made in the form of a cloak with a richly ornamented border or part border of a design called taniko. Feathers of various birds were woven into cloaks for persons of supreme importance and while those depicted in this section were manufactured after the arrival of Europeans, they are of considerable age, contain only feathers of endemic bird species and there is no reason to doubt, are faithful copies of pre-contact capes.

Early Maori migrants introduced a species of dog, the last descendant of which died in the late nineteenth century. This kuri was the only domestic animal the Maori possessed and was a valuable source of food. Strips of its cured skin were sewn on to a heavy backing of woven flax to make the most prized cloak of all.

PLATE 2/1 *Kilt or maro*
The amount of clothing worn by the early Maori could well have varied with the climatic changes known to have occurred in the last thousand years or so. The maro or kilt shown in this plate may well have been as much clothing as was ever required by the younger women during the summer.

Plates 2/1–2/5 by courtesy of Dominion Museum, Wellington.
Plates 2/6–2/8 by courtesy of Wanganui Public Museum.
Plates 2/9–2/11 by courtesy of Auckland War Memorial Museum.

PLATE 2/2 *Single rain cape*
The problem of remaining warm and dry concerned the pre-contact Maori as much as the present day New Zealander. Though not elegant and certainly not beautiful, the rain cape, as depicted in this plate, was serviceable and its manufacture relatively easy.

PLATE 2/3 *Dog skin cape*
The right to wear a rare and valuable cloak made from strips of the cured skin of the Maori dog or kuri was a guaranteed badge of high rank. This plate shows one of the very few remaining cloaks of this class still extant.

PLATE 2/4 *Multiple rain capes*
Like the ordinary man of today, the ancient Maori donned extra clothing as the need arose. The model in this plate gives an indication of the sensible thing to do in early New Zealand: if one rain cape did not keep out the rain, put on two, then three and so on, so that bulk and thickness made up for lack of water proofing.

PLATE 2/5 *Maori sleeping position*
A chronicler of an early voyage to New Zealand remarked that in the misty dawn he and his companions were amazed to see a circle of grassy tussocks, stand up and walk away. What had caused this amazement was the peculiar but highly practical sleeping position which Maori men adopted when night-fall caught them in the open.

PLATE 2/6 *Chieftainess dress*
There is little reliable information on pre-contact women's dress thus this plate moves into the realm of conjecture. It is however known that women of high rank were especially privileged in being allowed to dress more elaborately than the commoner. As a point of interest the lady who so kindly modelled these garments remarked that although a bitter Southerly wind was blowing the cloaks were very much warmer than the contemporary winter clothing she usually wore.

PLATE 2/7 *Feather cloak*
Many New Zealand native birds are endowed with brilliant plumage. The pre-contact Maori when weaving cloaks for persons of high status often locked the feathers of native birds into patterns on the outside of the garment. The example seen on this page is believed to be a fair representation of the appearance of such a cape.

PLATE 2/8 *Kiwi feather cloak*

The kiwi (Apteryx spp), a flightless bird of very great antiquity, is peculiar to New Zealand. The feathers of the kiwi lack the barbules need to lock together the feathers of a bird in flight and hence kiwi feathers are down-like and a favourite material for adding warmth and luxuriousness to fine cloaks. The particular example modelled in this plate is of post-European manufacture although as far as can be determined it has been made in the traditional manner from traditional materials, with the exception that a border design has been added. This extra embellishment on traditional form is typical of the beginning of the decline in classical formalism which followed European contact.

PLATES 2/9, 2/10 & 2/11 *Taniko patterns*
The plates shown on this page display a few of the many ingenious and highly artistic designs perfected by the Maori. These edge a cloak of fine flax fibre and the patterns are made by a system of finger weaving somewhat akin to plaiting. The weaving of flax materials was laborious, as the Maori used only the crudest technology for this purpose. The taniko borders were even more difficult to achieve and the patterns themselves are considered to have special significance, possibly religious, but certainly sociological.

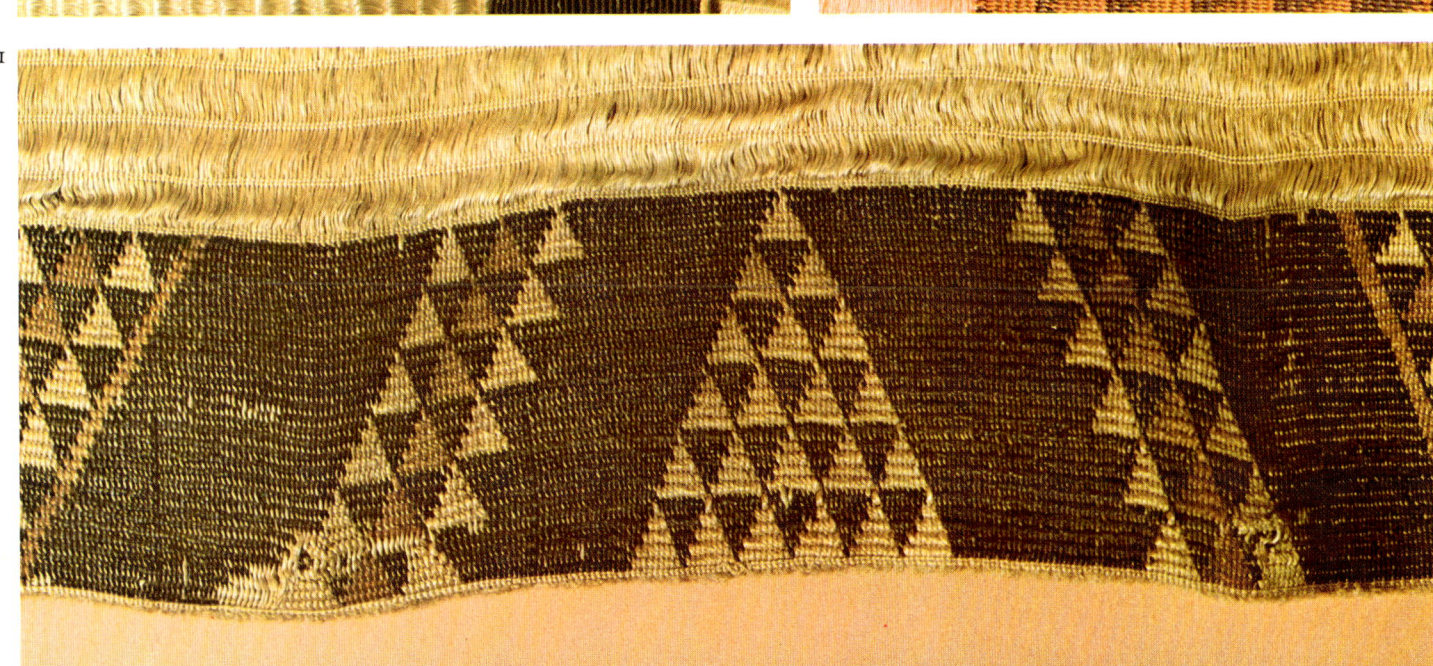

CHAPTER THREE

War and recreation

War to the Maori was indeed recreation, a form of sport carried out under firmly established rules and using a limited range of weapons. This is not to infer that the frequent inter-tribal battles were not sanguinary affairs. However it appears as though Maori warfare was seldom carried out for purposes other than those we of today would associate with a serious sporting fixture in which feeling among the players and supporters was running high.

Maori males spent a considerable portion of their time in grooming for battle. Their chosen weapons required a very high degree of physical fitness and were only effective by reason of considerable dexterity in their use. Missile weapons were never greatly used as far as is known, although there is some anthropological evidence to suggest that throwing spears, whip spears, slings and bows were at one stage or another known to the ancient Maori. From this it may be inferred that war was considered to be a contest of skill rather than the bloody business of win at all costs which is and has nearly always been, the approach of European races towards domination in battle.

A number of sites have been found which show clearly the manner of defence adopted by Maori military engineers in fortifying their villages. Captain Cook in the journal of his first visit gives high praise to the skill of the Maori in this respect and all evidence supports the belief that of all primitive people the Maori was especially skilled in defensive military works.

Preparations for war were ceremonious to the extreme and lasted far longer than the battles themselves. Invocations to the gods; strict observance of all the measures needed to propitiate evil influences; the composition of insulting ngeri to be chanted in the face of the enemy and such-like activities could occupy a whole community for weeks and were no doubt highly enjoyable social occasions which did not necessarily end in pitched warfare.

PLATE 3/1 *Bone club*
Weapons to a warrior race were of intense personal interest. This short stabbing club of whalebone displays a purity of artistic form much at variance with its overt purpose.

PLATE 3/2 *Stone stabbing club—wahaika*
The asymmetrical sickle shape of this Maori weapon has been beautifully executed in very hard stone. The patience and skill required to produce such an article, using other stones to first chip and then grind the shape, is considerable. The writer has handled a number of such weapons and continues to be amazed at the heft; the almost living feeling of the correct distribution of the balance, that these primitive craftsmen imparted to their artifacts.

PLATE 3/3 *Bone club—wahaika*
A first class example of a bone stabbing club is illustrated in this plate. The simple but highly sophisticated surface carving on this club is so typical of early Maori carving. Despite the flesh breaking niche cut into the striking edge this particular example is possibly a ceremonial club carried for much the same ornamental reasons as some European regiments issue swords to their mechanised troops.

Plates 3/1, 3/6, 3/7, 3/11–3/14, 3/16, 3/19, 3/20 by courtesy of Wanganui Public Museum.
Plates 3/2–3/5, 3/8–3/10, 3/17, 3/18 by courtesy of Dominion Museum, Wellington.
Plate 3/15 by courtesy of Auckland War Memorial Museum.

3/1

3/2   3/3

PLATE 3/4 *Bone stabbing club—kotiate*
Believed to have originated in pre-European times, the kotiate featured in this plate must have been borne in battle during the contact period, for the chip removed from the curve of the club was made by a musket ball.

PLATE 3/5 *Wooden stabbing club—kotiate*
The violin shape of this kotiate lends character to an otherwise broad, flat shape. It also had its practical use for the niches in the striking edge were more effective in splitting and lacerating the flesh of an enemy than a smooth flat edge.

PLATE 3/6 *Greenstone mere*
The delicate shape of the mere preserves the strength and toughness inherent in nephrite, essential to its purpose as a weapon of war, and demanding much of the artist who worked in this material. That the result is artistic as well as utilitarian is a tribute to his command of a difficult medium.

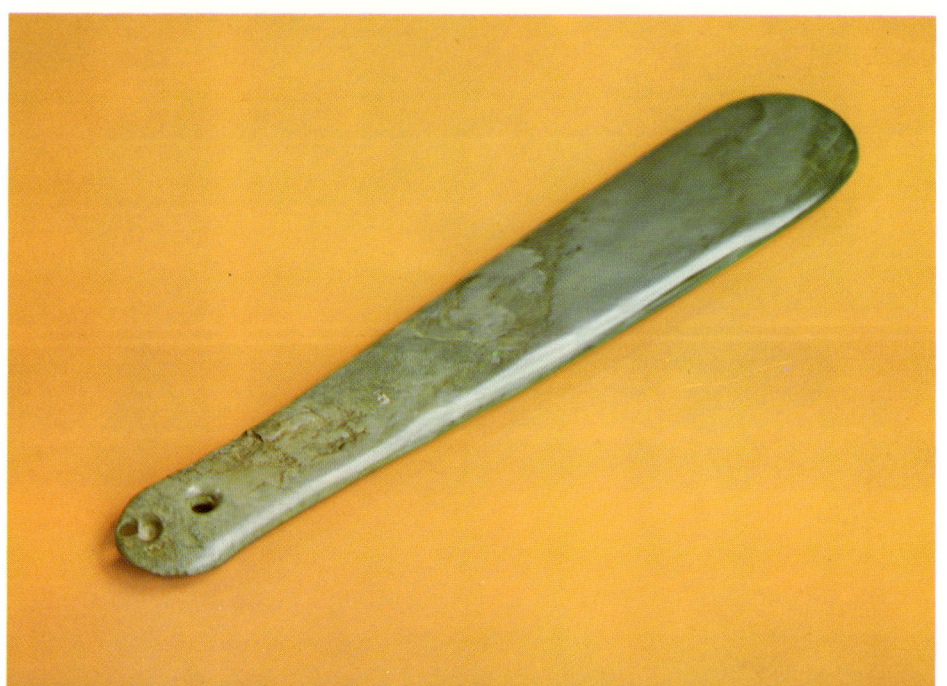

PLATE 3/7 *Two stone mere*
These two further examples of stone weapons give an indication of the inherent artistry and understanding of natural form so characteristic of primitive Maori workmanship.

PLATE 3/8 *Greenstone—mere pounamu*
Here is a wonderful example of what was probably the most prized weapon of the Maori warrior, the stabbing club made from the tough, hard nephrite of New Zealand. A pounamu (nephrite) club would not shatter when struck heavily by another club while the owner was warding off a blow. In this example the tau, or wrist cord, designed to prevent the club being struck away from the user, is of recent production, but is probably a close approximation of the original tau as fitted.

PLATE 3/9 *Stone stabbing club—patu onewa*
The Maori word onewa refers to a number of hard, close grained varieties of stone. All of these stones were inferior to the tough grained nephrite, pounamu or greenstone, from which superior weapons were made, as onewa being more crystalline and hence shorter in the grain than the rather fibrous structure of nephrite, would shatter when brought into heavy contact with a club made of the latter material.

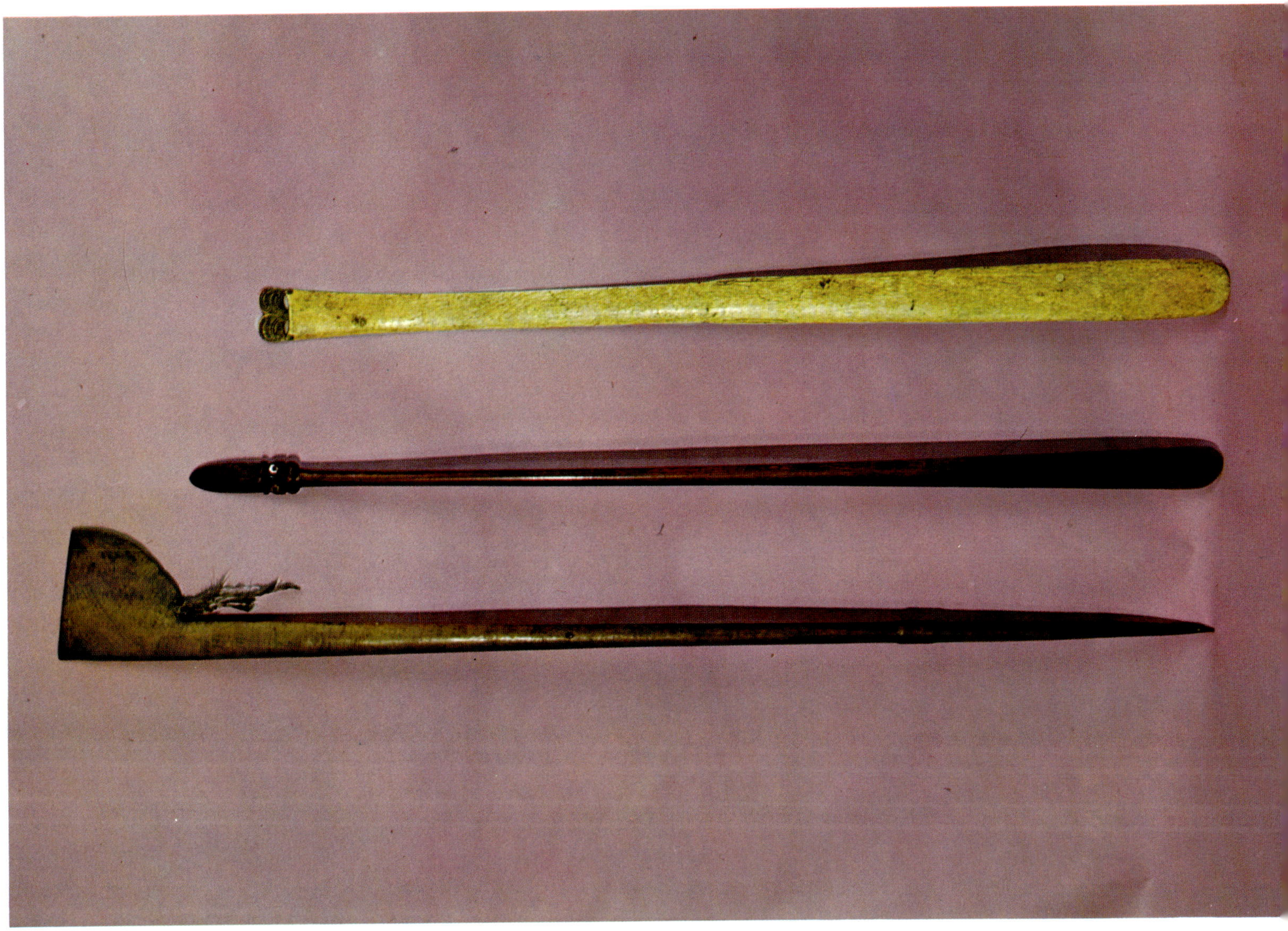

PLATE 3/10—*Whale-bone pouwhenua, wooden taiaha and wooden tewhatewha*

The above three club-spears are representative of the longer hand weapons of the Maori. They were all used by gripping in the middle and alternately thrusting with the point or clubbing with the blade. The tewhatewha is not an axe, for the blow was struck with the straight edge; the blade extension being provided to add extra weight and balance at the end of the weapon.

PLATE 3/11 *Wooden clubs—taiaha*

These three examples of long-handled wooden clubs are light in weight, flexible and not particularly strong. Their effective use depended upon agility and long hours of exercise and practice.

3/12

3/13

3/14

PLATE 3/12 *Shell trumpet—putatara*
Basically fashioned from the large tropical conch shell found in the Northern sections of New Zealand the putatara was not a musical instrument but a signalling device, possibly used in war. The plaited cord shown in the plate is of recent manufacture.

PLATE 3/13 *Long trumpet—pukaea*
This pukaea is nearly six feet in length and made from hollowed sections of wood lashed together. With its bell-shaped mouth and its great length it emits a sound capable of carrying over considerable distances.

PLATE 3/14 *Short wooden trumpet*
An alternative and shorter form of wooden trumpet is shown in this plate and displays the ingenuity of the artisan. Such an instrument as this was in all probability the type carried by Maori raiding or skirmishing parties and used much in the same way as modern soldiers use radio.

PLATE 3/15 *Puppet*
The pre-contact Maori is known to have manufactured a variety of dolls or puppets in wood; their actual usage is not now known.

PLATE 3/16 *Small wooden figure*
In contrast to the high degree of realism of the wooden figure with moveable arms depicted in the last plate, this figure is very much simpler in execution and more stylised in form. Nevertheless its very simplicity and the use made of the natural form of the wood from which it was carved, give it its own appeal.

3/15

3/16

Maori Music

To people raised in the Western tradition of major and minor musical scales with an eight note octave and a more or less well defined harmonic content, it is difficult to equate Maori chanting with music as such, for the pre-contact Maori used none of these devices in his songs.

Despite the gross difference between the music of the two cultures, the voices of the pre-contact Maori were described by Captain Cook 'as remarkably mellow and soft'. This virtue and the innate sense of rhythm which seems to be the birthright of those of Maori blood, has allowed the descendants of the early Maori to distinguish themselves in many fields of contemporary music, in particular, the vocal arts.

The primitive Maori had some elementary percussion instruments, (a tapping-stick—pakuru, and wood and bone castanets), but no drums. The most important of his instruments were the various forms of flute as illustrated here. The most common flute (koauau) is from three to eight inches in length; open at both ends; with three holes drilled along the top and when blown across one end can produce six half-tones in consecutive order.

PLATE 3/18 *Long flute—putorino*
This long flute shows the artistic ingenuity of the Maori artisan who fitted his carved design into the restrictions of his instrument in such a way as to be able to naturally carve the outlet as lips with the rest of the facial features falling into place. The long flute, some fifteen inches in length, is reputed to be able to carry messages over long distances.

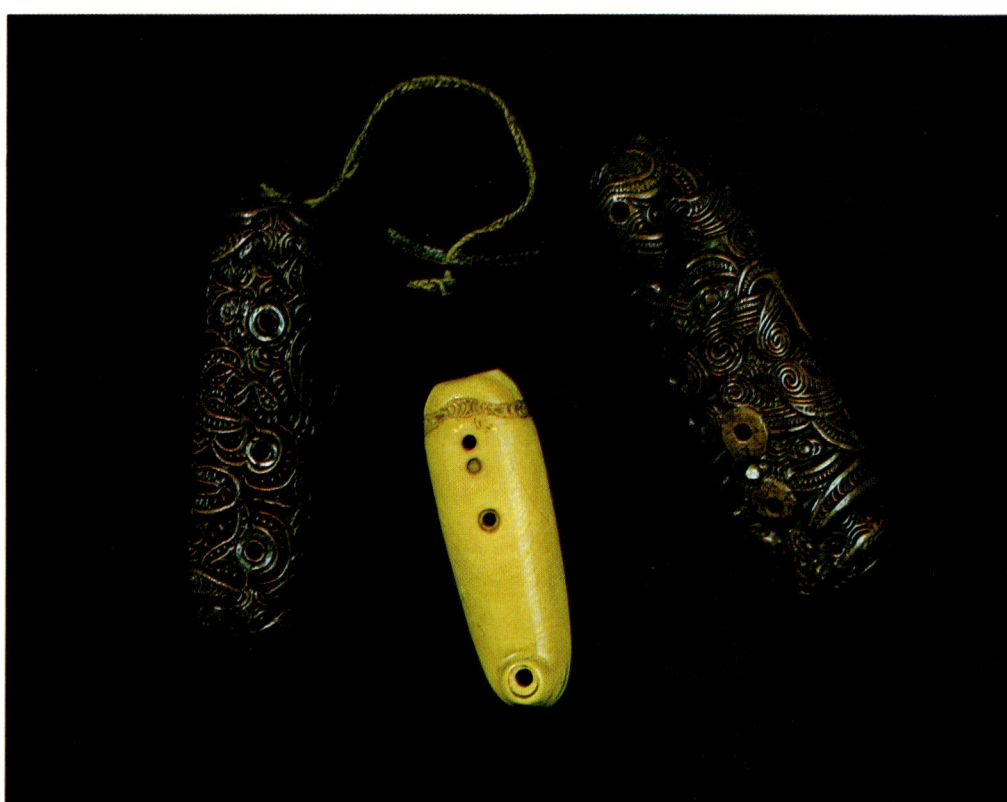

PLATE 3/17 *Short flutes—koauau*
This group of three typical pre-contact period short flutes gives an indication of the carved embellishments said to add magical powers to the music. Two of the instruments shown are carved from wood whilst the central flute is made from bone.

PLATE 3/19 *Spinning tops*
It is always difficult to decide whether artifacts, which we of our generation would regard as play-things, were so used by the Maori. However the tops shown in this plate bear resemblance to the common whip top of Europe and in all probability had no other purpose than the amusement of the young and even perhaps the elders of the Maori community.

PLATE 3/20 *Poi*
The Maori of old in his musical expression apparently accompanied his chants with bodily movements. To give additional action he used poi, which are balls of vegetable fibre on the end of a string, and swung them in unison with the chanting. These are believed to be nineteenth century types of poi, but have been included for sake of completeness.

3/19

3/20

CHAPTER FOUR

Ancestor reverence

As mentioned previously, the primitive Maori was completely and simultaneously involved in his real and spirit worlds. The importance of his mana and the involvement of his ancestors in this most momentous facet of his life have been discussed in a previous section. His deep spirituality and his need to sanctify and venerate his ancestors made inevitable the urge to deify many of the personages of his remote past.

It was the Maori belief that certain articles had the power to attract and hold inhabitants of the spirit world. From this belief arose the natural assumption that the most beneficent spirits would be those of ancestors who, because of their outstanding deeds in the real world, would have special authority in the spirit world. Hence arose the cult of preservation of the human head.

The preserving of heads was a skilled, if somewhat macabre art. A specially built oven was used to thoroughly cook the head and then all the fleshy portions and the eyes were removed; the eye holes were sewn up and then the specimen was subjected to alternate smoking and oiling.

The head was the most sacred portion of the body and a stylised replica in stone or wood was sometimes substituted for an actual preserved head of an ancestor. It is curious that no attempt appears to have been made to introduce realism into the artist's work. All primitive Maori art forms, while varied in basic character, have in common this stylised abstraction which ranges from the slightly distorted to an almost completely dehumanised form.

Plates 4/1–4/5, 4/9, 4/12–4/14, 4/16 by courtesy of Auckland War Memorial Museum.

Plates 4/6–4/8, 4/10, 4/11, 4/15 by courtesy of Wanganui Public Museum.

PLATE 4/1 *Human head*
A strange medium for the practice of art is the human skin, but the Maori was not alone among primitive people in so using the human face. The curvilinear design of human tattooing has its own particular grace. That the process was painful and the operation difficult of execution is certain, but the result was an art form which is considered to be peculiar to early New Zealand alone.

PLATE 4/2 *Head in pumice*
Soft pumice stone is common to large areas of New Zealand and very easy to work. The degree of realism imparted by the artist to the free-standing sculpture of this plate possibly indicates that it represents a well known and recent ancestor.

PLATE 4/3 *Hollow sculpture*
This hollow wooden sculpture, in which the bones of a dead kinsman were probably placed, undoubtedly pays tribute to his memory and attributes.

PLATES 4/4 & 4/5 *Funeral casket and detail*
These plates show a highly imaginative and artistically presented depiction of the spirit of a departed ancestor in the form of a wooden bone box.

PLATE 4/6 *God sticks*
The early Maori worshipped no images but their belief that certain objects or totems had the power to attract and hold beneficent spirits was strong. Such objects are often referred to as god sticks.

PLATE 4/7 *Three god sticks*
The three further examples of god sticks shown in this plate indicate the variety of modes in which the Maori artist could work. Thus is the lie given to those who claim that Maori art is stylized and stereotyped.

PLATE 4/8 *Religious figure*
This larger example of the class of art work discussed in the last two plates is of considerable merit in once again displaying the sympathy which existed between the Maori artist and the medium in which he worked.

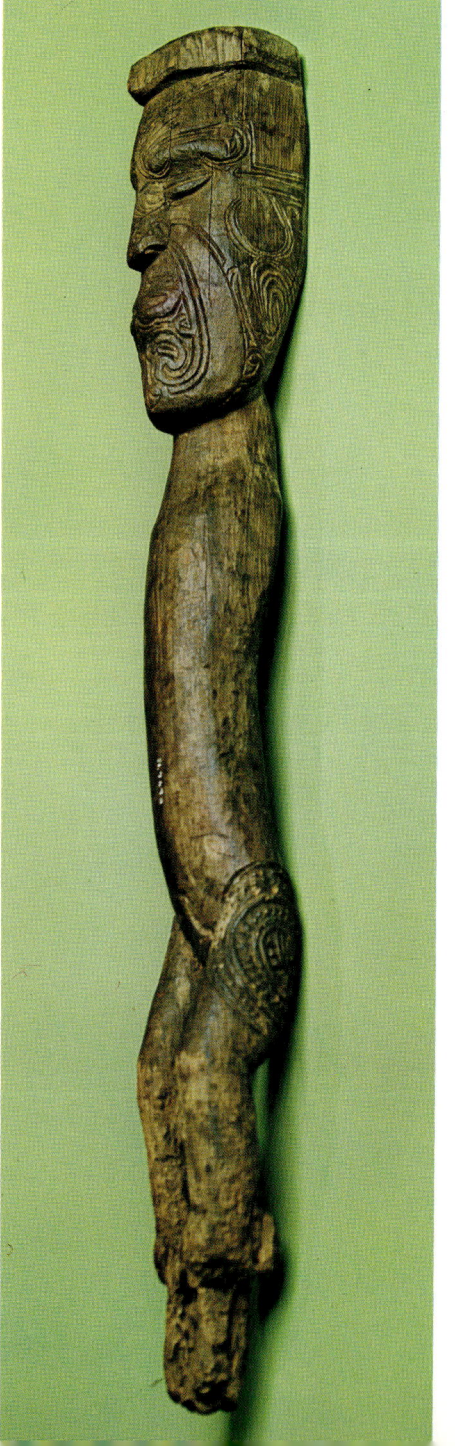

PLATE 4/9 *Stone figure*
An elaborately carved free-standing stone figure is shown in this plate. The spiral pattern, which, in post-European times became the predominant motif in Maori art is here shown as a simple spiral curve.

PLATE 4/10 *Stone carving—rongo*
This plate represents a stone carving of considerable age but one which in its simplicity of shape and the retention of the stony quality of the medium would be well in keeping with the work of many contemporary artists.

PLATE 4/11 *Pierced wooden composition*
Typical of much early Maori work is the flexibility of execution, the balance of composition and the degree of movement imparted to wooden carving. The pierced work and the accompanying figures produce an admirably balanced design.

PLATE 4/12 *Patetonga roof piece*
One of the most celebrated and possibly the largest known piece of pre-contact Maori workmanship is shown in this plate. Details of the figure work have been shown already in 'The Imaginative Maori' and here the progression from a formalized human figure, shown full face in the centre, to the abstraction of the outer end can be clearly seen.

PLATE 4/13 *Slab carving*
A somewhat atypical example of early Maori workmanship can be seen in this plate. The design is simple, overall somewhat grotesque, and yet the repetition of the basic design elements lends an air of importance to the composition.

PLATE 4/14 *Wood carving in detail*
Here in juxtaposition can be seen a very fine example of the effect of the side facing and front facing figures. The profile figures are abstracted to become manaia, and the full face figures, when fully stylised, tiki.

PLATE 4/15 *Heitiki*
The New Zealand Maori tiki, or more correctly heitiki, has come to be regarded as almost the symbol of the country. Certainly it was a very popular personal ornament in early times judging by the number rendered in greenstone. The esoteric significance of this type of stylised human figure is not known.

PLATE 4/16 *Greenstone manaia*
The subject of this plate is designed to be worn as a personal ornament or charm. The humanistic characterization has been almost entirely abstracted until the representation assumes an almost birdlike character. This may be deliberate but can also be explained away in terms of the ultimate stylization of the human profile.

CHAPTER FIVE

Domestic art forms

This section begins with the artifacts used in the collection and preparation of food which the Maori obtained from three main sources; from their agriculture; from the rivers, lakes and ocean and from the forest in the form of plant foods and native birds.

The early voyagers, brought with them the Maori dog, the kuri, and they also introduced a species of rat. Fish, sharks, eels, mollusca, crustaceans, birds, rats, occasionally a dog and sometimes a man, were the only source of animal protein, and through the long winter all were difficult to obtain. The Maori showed considerable ingenuity in the storage of birds and rats, usually preserving them in their own fat. Special vessels were made specifically for this purpose.

The Maori had no knowledge either of pottery making or metal working and substituted wooden bowls or hollowed gourd plants as containers for liquids and food.

The act of eating was surrounded by a degree of religious ceremonial, particularly with persons of high rank, who were sometimes forbidden to feed themselves. Hence the need for feeding funnels and feeding spears to allow a second person to administer food without contact being made between the two persons.

Little is known as to the degree personal ornaments were used and even what particular significance wearing of them had. However various types of bodily ornaments were common and the most significant are illustrated in this section.

Plates 5/1, 5/4, 5/6, 5/7, 5/9, 5/15–5/17, 5/19–5/21 by courtesy of Wanganui Public Museum.

Plates 5/2, 5/3, 5/5, 5/11, 5/12, 5/22–5/24 by courtesy of Auckland War Memorial Museum.

Plates 5/8, 5/10, 5/13, 5/14, 5/18 by courtesy of Dominion Museum, Wellington.

PLATE 5/1 *Totara bark basket*
The totara tree (Podocarpus totara) is a large species of a tree family of long lineage. It was the favourite carving and structural timber of the Maori and its tough, stringy bark was used to make baskets of the type shown in this plate.

PLATE 5/2 *Wooden bowl*
The instinctive love of form and the inherent balance imparted by the Maori to his simplest artifacts is shown to advantage in this example of a pre-contact period food bowl.

PLATE 5/3 *Carved stone bowl*
Cut from comparatively easily worked soapstone the bowl shown in this plate displays an economy of design and an elegance of form as beautiful as it is utilitarian.

PLATE 5/4 *Gourds*
The gourd plant is a member of the same general group of plants as the pumpkin. Distribution of gourds is worldwide, largely owing to the usefulness of its fruit as containers. Undoubtedly the earliest Maori settlers introduced the plant to their new homeland.

PLATE 5/5 *Carved gourd*
This plate depicts a domestic vessel which has been embellished with a clever geometric design. It is almost contemporary in its concept and the artistry is of a high order.

PLATE 5/6 *Necked gourd*
The pre-contact Maori used the fruits of a variety of the gourd plant as domestic utensils. On occasions a carved wooden neck was fitted to a gourd in order to extend its capacity and make the pouring of liquids easier.

PLATE 5/7 *Bird container*
Birds gave the Maori a convenient source of animal protein for their diet. The container shown in this plate is a fairly typical example of the storage vessels in which birds were preserved.

PLATE 5/8 *Feeding vessel*
High personages became, at times, religiously untouchable or tapu. During such periods they were not allowed to feed themselves and the wooden bowl shown (underside) is an example of the type of vessel in which food was delivered to a person under tapu.

PLATE 5/9 *Feeding spear*
Used in conjunction with the bowl of plate 5/8 this bone feeding spear or tirou was used by a slave or other person of low rank to convey food from the feeding bowl to the personage under tapu.

PLATE 5/10 *Feeding funnel*
The feeding of liquid foods to a tohunga or high ranking chief under tapu was carried out by a second person pouring the liquid via a funnel of this type into the mouth of the victim. One says victim for although it was usually an honour to be under tapu, this method of being fed must have been unpleasant, to say the least.

PLATE 5/11 *Embellished stone—marutuahu*
A stone object of special appeal. The surface carved pattern has a strong vibrant motif and the sense of life-force imparted by the artist is exceptionally clear.

PLATES 5/12, 5/13 & 5/14   *Feather boxes—whakahuia*

Whakahuia: the Maori name indicates that these finely ornamented wooden storage chests were used for the keeping of huia feathers. The huia was a native bird of distinctive black feathers tipped with white, and was the apparent mark of rank when worn in the hair. The huia became extinct in post-European times. Whakahuia of authentic pre-contact times are rare and these are believed to be genuine examples. Owing to their shape feather boxes had special appeal to the Victorian traders of early colonial times and large numbers of post-European examples, elaborately carved with steel tools, are in existence.

PLATE 5/15 *Ear pendants*
Sketches produced by early European voyagers showed that ear ornaments of one type or another were commonly worn by both sexes. The three examples shown in this plate are made of nephrite.

PLATE 5/17 *Personal ornaments*
This plate sets out yet further examples of articles intended to be used as ornaments. The pendant in the bottom left corner with its simple spiral shape is of particular appeal and represents many hours of patient work in the shaping of the hard tough stone from which it was made.

PLATE 5/16 *Greenstone pendants*
The pre-European Maori was fond of personal adornment and the symmetry and proportions of the pendants shown in this plate display his love of beautiful form.

PLATE 5/18 *Man's dress comb—heru*
The comb as used by the Maori was not a practical implement for grooming the hair. As a well known sketch by Parkinson shows (the artist who accompanied Cook on his first voyage) the Maori male used combs as a decorative item fixed into his hair top knot (putiki).

PLATE 5/19 *Wooden combs*
Further evidence that the combs used by the early Maori had little practical value for dressing the hair. The Maori male commonly wore his hair long, tied into a top knot in the centre of the hair, and with the ends left loose.

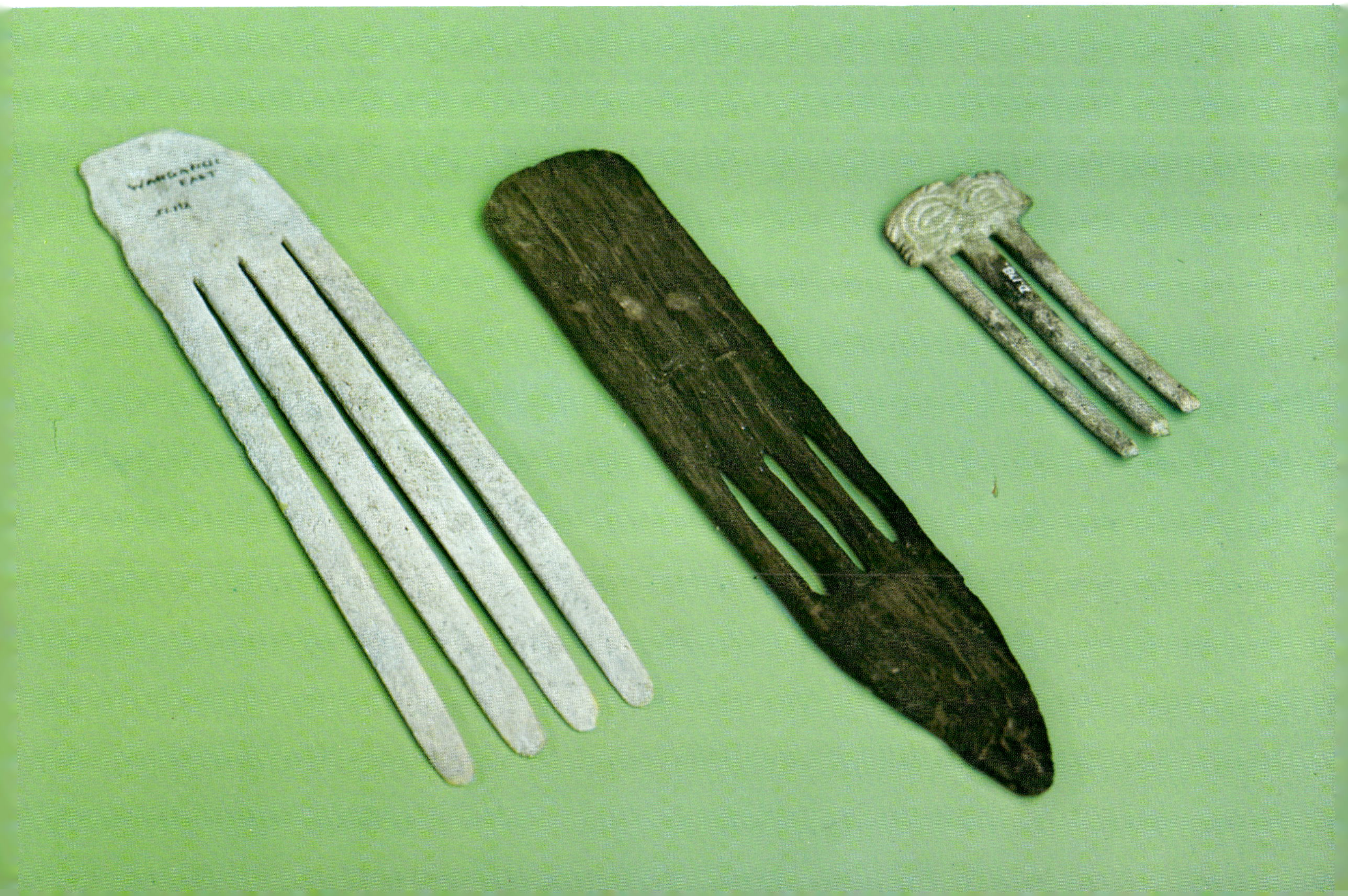

5/20

5/21

PLATE 5/20 *Plaited belt*
Some of the more puritanical members of eighteenth-century expeditions to New Zealand complained in their diaries of the lack of modesty of the New Zealand natives. This is understandable when it is realised that a man wearing only the belt shown in this plate was often considered to be adequately clothed.

PLATE 5/21 *War belt*
Game or not, Maori warfare was a serious business and the most cherished and best personal articles were reserved for use at such times. The artistically patterned belt displayed here could well be what a well dressed warrior would have worn.

PLATE 5/22 *Pumice box*
This delightfully carved object is fairly obviously a storage box, perhaps it may even be a vessel in which tattooing pigment was kept. However, although its original usage may not be known there is no question of the whimsical charm of the object.

PLATES 5/23 & 5/24 *Greenstone carvings* The plates on these pages are shown together so that the variety in design achieved by individual artists, even when using the same basic motif can be easily compared.

CHAPTER SIX

Art outdoors

PLATE 6/1 *Stone face*
This rudely carved rough stone head has a strange whimsical appeal. Quite atypical of most known pre-contact sculpture the happy countenance, quite devoid of menace, seems to fit ill with preconceived ideas of Maori sculpture.

Plates 6/1, 6/3, 6/15–6/18 by courtesy of Auckland War Memorial Museum.
Plates 6/2, 6/4–6/9, 6/11–6/14, 6/24 by courtesy of Wanganui Public Museum.
Plates 6/10, 6/19–6/23 by courtesy of Dominion Museum, Wellington.

The Maori of old lived frugally and well by the exercise of much ingenuity and considerable effort in a country not naturally endowed with a plentitude of ready food. The Maori belief in the efficacy of spiritual intervention to aid him in his struggle for existence caused him to embellish even his humblest tools with sacred symbolism in order to encourage favourable spirit guidance and control of his labour. Such was the natural artistry of these people that with very few exceptions there is an aesthetic quality apparent in the simplest artifacts.

The Maori was a slash and burn agriculturist, burning off the bush; turning over the ash-enriched soil with a pointed implement, a ko, fitted with a footrest; pounding the broken clods and planting his food plants.

Many of his artifacts, including his meticulously executed ocean-going canoes, were carved from wood. Major wood working operations were carried out using as tools the various sizes of adzes he made from rock, in particular the hard, tough greenstone nephrite which he called pounamu.

With the aid of his canoes he fished the seas around the coast, using seine nets, drag nets, line and troll fishing as well as dredges and rakes for shell-fish; baskets and pots for fish, crustaceans and eels; spears, clubs and weirs for fish and eels. From the forest came the timber for his artifacts and also from the forest he took the many birds which formed a main source of animal protein for inland tribes. Birds were speared using long slender simple spears; snared by a variety of ingenious devices; caught by hand with the aid of decoys and less often netted.

The carved work of the canoe prow and stern pieces shown in this section are worthy of special note. While it is by no means sure that intricate carving was commonly executed for use in buildings or pallisades prior to contact with Europeans, it is certain that carved canoe prows and stern pieces were in normal usage and some of the very finest examples extant were originally executed for this purpose.

PLATE 6/2 *Ko tread*
The loving workmanship and sheer artistry with which the primitive Maori artist embellished his humblest artifacts is seen to advantage in this plate. The ko or digging spear was normally fitted with a foot rest and these two examples of foot rests show a superior artistic integrity.

PLATE 6/3 *Boundary marker*
One of the few inalienable rights of Maori tribal ownership was to land and tribal territories were marked carefully along the boundaries. The beautiful chevroned form of the boundary marker stone in this plate at one time no doubt marked the territorial division between two tribes.

PLATES 6/4, 6/5 & 6/6 *Stone adze heads*
The three plates on this page feature a varied selection of stone adze heads. The adze was the favourite instrument for timber working, the stone head being lashed to the haft with flax cordage. As objects of three dimensional beauty these tools display an innate love of shape and balance.

PLATE 6/7 *Hafted adze*
Pre-contact Maori artifacts had to have aesthetic as well as utilitarian value. Not only was a tool required to do the job well but it also had to look well too. This requirement had religious overtones since beautiful objects were pleasing to the gods.

PLATE 6/8 *Bird snare*
The teeming bird life of the New Zealand rain forests was apparently an inexhaustable food source and bird snaring an art. The cordage shown in the plate is modern but of a type known to be manufactured by the primitive Maori, the snare itself is very old.

PLATE 6/9 *Spear heads and fishhook*
It is curious that the Maori apparently did not use spears in his warfare for there are numerous examples extant of spear heads similar to these examples. Fashioned from bone, sometimes human bone, and affixed to the end of long slender spears, these brutally barbed points were used for the spearing of large birds high up in the upper canopy of the dense forests.

PLATE 6/10 *Shark tooth saw*
This illustration shows a saw made from shark teeth, pierced for lashing to a wood backing with vegetable fibre cordage. These saws were apparently used for the cutting of flesh, usually during cannibal feasts. The curious fact is that there is no evidence that the Maori ever applied these saws to the cutting of wood although such devices are reasonably effective when so used.

PLATE 6/11 *Stake maul*
For such a mundane object this wooden club or maul, presumably used for driving stakes into the bed of streams to hold a weir, has a curiously graceful form.

PLATE 6/12 *Eel killing club*
Matching the aesthetic qualities of the subject of plate 6/11 is this club used for the final dispatch of trapped eels. All such clubs have an overall resemblance and a typical shapely form.

PLATE 6/13 *Mussel rake*
Used for the dredging of the edible mussel which grows in quantity on the New Zealand coasts, this dredger shows the high point of pre-contact Maori technology in one direction. Although the implement could have been equally efficient in a more clumsy form the artisan who made it chose his timbers so as to retain symmetrical appeal.

PLATE 6/14 *Fishing tackle*
To the coast living Maori of ancient times fishing was a way of life. An ingenious variety of fishing gear was in use and shown in the plate are two hooks, a troll and a line sinker. Yet again the Maori's natural love of beauty is reflected in the manufacture of everyday artifacts.

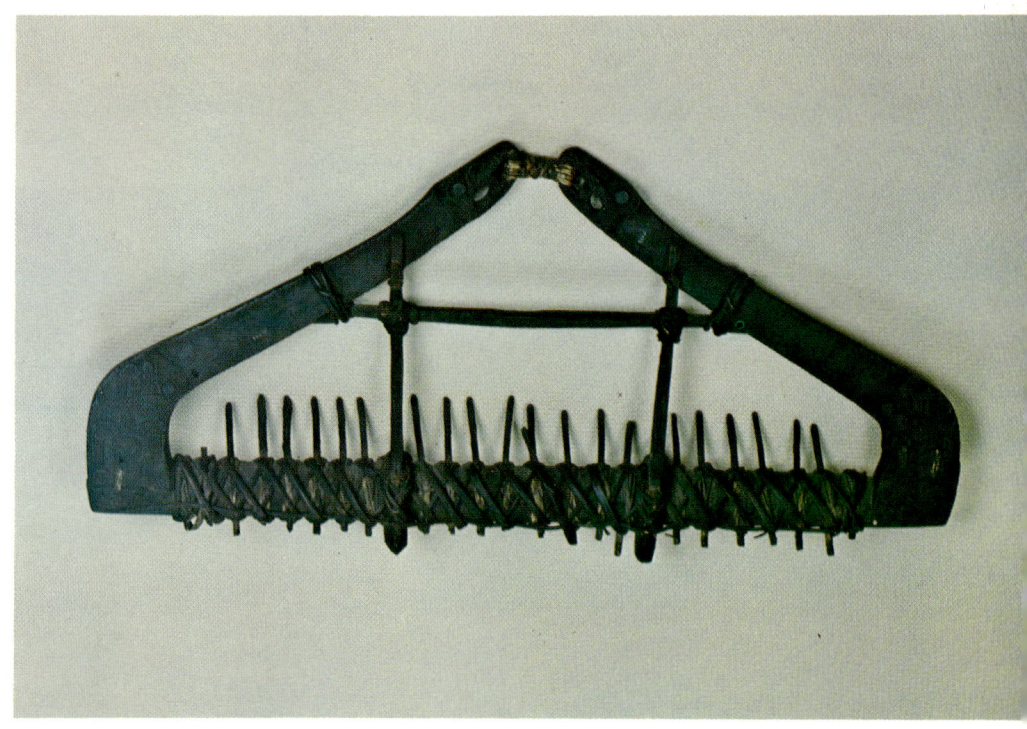

6/15

PLATE 6/15 *Stone sinker*
The classical simplicity of the incised carving of this simple stone sinker gives it a timeless quality quite in keeping with contemporary modes of art. The interlocked double spiral design is believed by some ethnologists to have some reference to the curled lips of a mythical sea monster.

PLATE 6/16 *Line sinker*
A Grecian purity of form is seen in the simple lines of this artifact. Any modern artist would be proud to achieve similar results with such economy of design.

PLATE 6/17 *Figured sinker*
Here a natural configuration of stone has been fashioned to give a semblance of two human figures joined back to back. This fishing line sinker displays a wealth of artistic imagination and a natural command of the medium in which it was worked.

6/17

6/16

PLATE 6/18 *Canoe prow*
The degree of realism of the carving shown in this plate is completely out of character with the style of decoration used for Maori canoe prows. There is no question of its authenticity but the style is so unusual that its origin has given cause for speculation.

PLATE 6/19 *Canoe paddle*
The pointed leaf-shaped blade of this canoe paddle is typical of the paddles of the Maori. Beautifully balanced with an inherently simple design, and with an almost complete lack of embellishment, this artifact has a classical appeal.

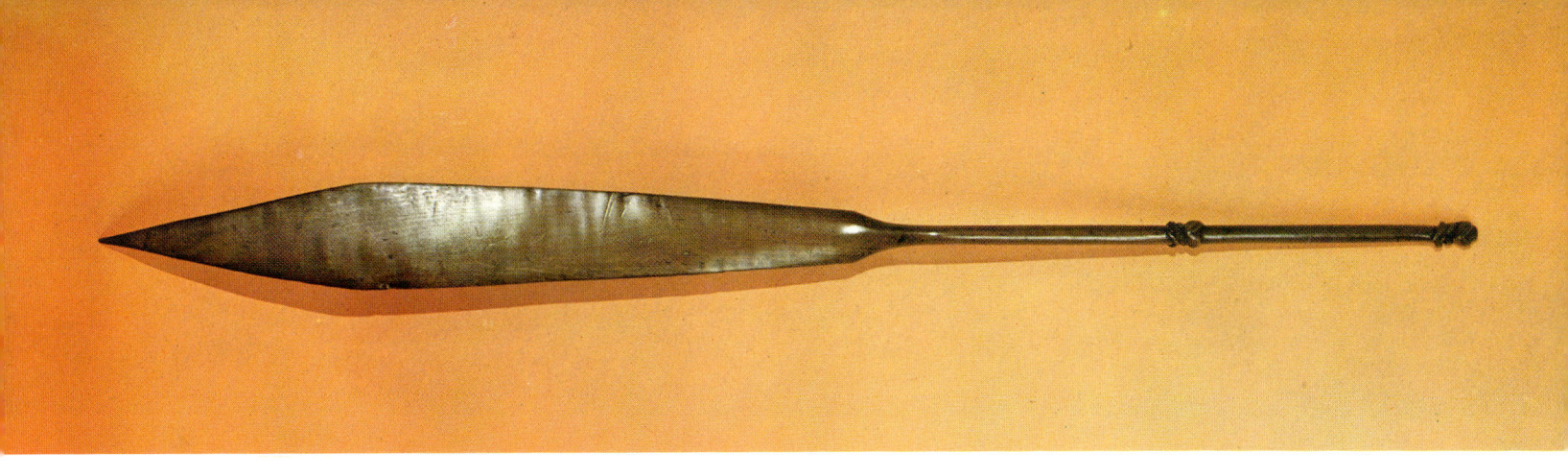

PLATE 6/20 *Canoe bailer—tata*
Strictly a utilitarian artifact, the shape of this canoe bailer is dictated by the need to rid a canoe of water speedily and efficiently. It is also a work of art, for the placement of the rich carving complements the form and adds interest to what could otherwise be an unattractive object.

PLATE 6/21 *Canoe prow*
A magnificent example of pre-contact Maori artistry is depicted in this canoe prow. The carving is not large but the balance and symmetry of the pierced carving and the detail carried out with stone implements ranks the work as very great art.

PLATE 6/22 *Canoe prow—pattern detail*
The intricate pierced work; the detail of the spiral pattern and repetitive motif which supplements the spiral is clearly shown in this canoe prow detail.

PLATE 6/23 *Canoe prow figure*
The figure shown here is the head of the winged three dimensional figure from which flows the design of the canoe prow in plate 6/21.

PLATE 6/24 *Canoe stern piece*
It is probable that the high point of pre-European Maori wood carving was reached in the elaborate but delicately incised carving of the prow and stern pieces of Maori war canoes. The earliest voyagers to New Zealand remark in their journals on the spectacular nature of the work and this plate is another typical example of those carvings still extant today.